Trace Letters

Brighter Child®
An imprint of Carson-Dellosa Publishing, LLC
P.O. Box 35665
Greensboro, NC 27425-5665

carsondellosa.com

ISBN 978-1-62057-444-7

10-250157784

Writing Tools and Safety

Using Writing Tools

Here are some tips to teach your child how to hold a pencil correctly and use it skillfully.

- Demonstrate how to pinch the writing utensil between your thumb and index finger and let it rest on the third finger. Encourage your child to mimic you.

- At this stage, your child may switch hand preference daily. Allow your child plenty of opportunities to experiment with using either hand. He or she will naturally establish a dominant hand.

- Let your child experiment with different writing instruments like crayons, markers, and pencils. Then, introduce pens, chalk, and paint.

- Some manufacturers make large crayons and colored pencils specifically for little hands. Large utensils are not a must, but they may be helpful for your child's first writing attempts.

Safety First

Here are some tips to make your child's first writing experiences pleasant and safe:

- Select markers, crayons, and colored pencils that are child friendly. Look for a label that says "Non Toxic and Washable."

- Remind your child that crayons, markers, pencils, and paint are for paper, not walls.

- Use a large piece of paper or a vinyl tablecloth to cover the space where you are working.

- Keep wipes or paper towels handy so you can clean marker from your child's hands.

A Is for Apple

Directions: Say the letter name out loud and have your child repeat you. What other words our child think of that start with the same sound as *apple*? Have your child trace the letters with his or her finger before using a pencil to complete the activity.

Trace a letter.

A is for apple.

B Is for Ball

Directions: Say the letter name out loud and have your child repeat you. What other words can your child think of that start with the same sound as *ball*? Have your child trace the letters with his or her finger before using a pencil to complete the activity.

Trace a letter.

B B B B B

B is for ball.

C Is for Car

Directions: Say the letter name out loud and have your child repeat you. What other words can your child think of that start with the same sound as *car*? Have your child trace the letters with his or her finger before using a pencil to complete the activity.

Trace a letter.

C C C C C

C **is for** car.

D Is for Dog

Directions: Say the letter name out loud and have your child repeat you. What other words can your child think of that start with the same sound as *dog*? Have your child trace the letters with his or her finger before using a pencil to complete the activity.

Trace a letter.

D is for dog.

E Is for Egg

Directions: Say the letter name out loud and have your child repeat you. What other words can your child think of that start with the same sound as *egg*? Have your child trace the letters with his or her finger before using a pencil to complete the activity.

Trace a letter.

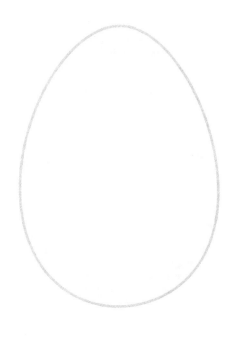

E is for egg.

ACTIVITY 6

F Is for Football

Directions: Say the letter name out loud and have your child repeat you. What other words can your child think of that start with the same sound as *football*? Have your child trace the letters with his or her finger before using a pencil to complete the activity.

Trace a letter.

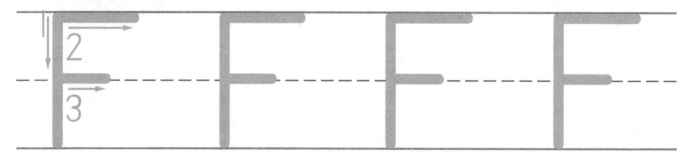

F is for football.

G Is for Guitar

Directions: Say the letter name out loud and have your child repeat you. What other words can your child think of that start with the same sound as *guitar*? Have your child trace the letters with his or her finger before using a pencil to complete the activity.

Trace a letter.

G G G G

G is for guitar.

H **Is for Hammer**

Directions: Say the letter name out loud and have your child repeat you. What other words can your child think of that start with the same sound as *hammer*? Have your child trace the letters with his or her finger before using a pencil to complete the activity.

Trace a letter.

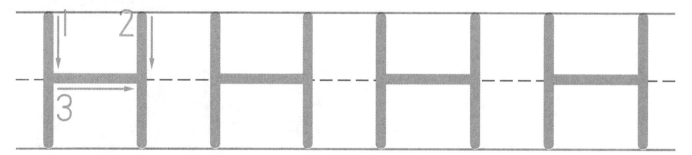

H is for hammer.

I Is for Ice Cream

Directions: Say the letter name out loud and have your child repeat you. What other words can your child think of that start with the same sound as *ice cream*? Have your child trace the letters with his or her finger before using a pencil to complete the activity.

Trace a letter.

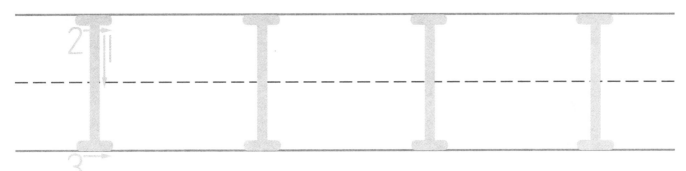

I **is for** ice cream.

J **Is for Jelly Bean**

Directions: Say the letter name out loud and have your child repeat you. What other words can your child think of that start with the same sound as *jelly bean*? Have your child trace the letters with his or her finger before using a pencil to complete the activity.

Trace a letter.

J J J J J

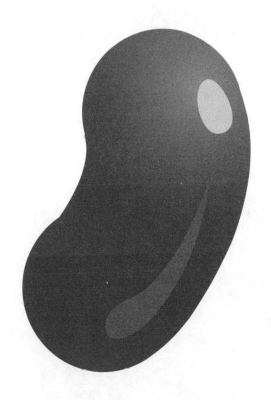

J **is for** jelly bean.

 **ACTIVITY 11**

K Is for Kangaroo

Directions: Say the letter name out loud and have your child repeat you. What other words can your child think of that start with the same sound as *kangaroo*? Have your child trace the letters with his or her finger before using a pencil to complete the activity.

Trace a letter.

K K K K

K is for **kangaroo.**

L Is for Lemon

Directions: Say the letter name out loud and have your child repeat you. What other words can your child think of that start with the same sound as *lemon*? Have your child trace the letters with his or her finger before using a pencil to complete the activity.

Trace a letter.

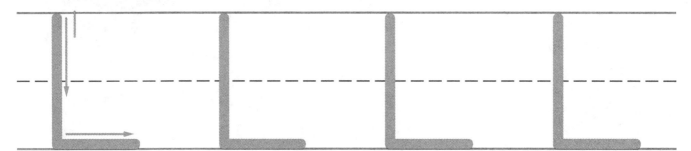

L is for lemon.

ACTIVITY 13

M Is for Mitten

Directions: Say the letter name out loud and have your child repeat you. What other words can your child think of that start with the same sound as *mitten*? Have your child trace the letters with his or her finger before using a pencil to complete the activity.

Trace a letter.

M **is for** mitten**.**

N Is for Nest

Directions: Say the letter name out loud and have your child repeat you. What other words can your child think of that start with the same sound as *nest*? Have your child trace the letters with his or her finger before using a pencil to complete the activity.

Trace a letter.

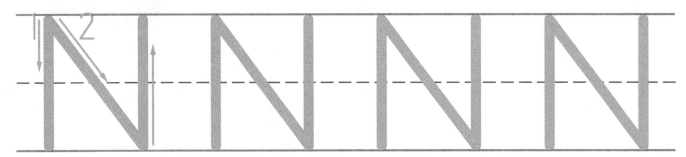

N is for nest.

O Is for Orange

Directions: Say the letter name out loud and have your child repeat you. What other words can your child think of that start with the same sound as *orange*? Have your child trace the letters with his or her finger before using a pencil to complete the activity.

Trace a letter.

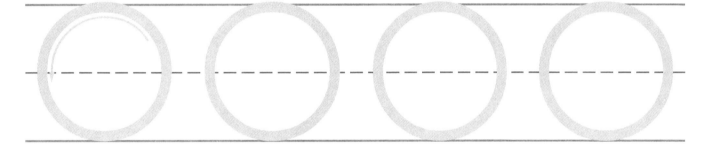

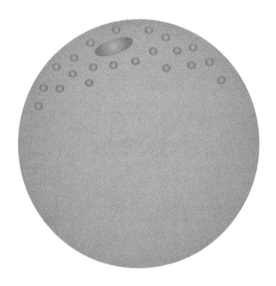

O **is for** orange**.**

P Is for Pear

Directions: Say the letter name out loud and have your child repeat you. What other words can your child think of that start with the same sound as *pear*? Have your child trace the letters with his or her finger before using a pencil to complete the activity.

Trace a letter.

P P P P P

P is for pear.

Q Is for Quilt

Directions: Say the letter name out loud and have your child repeat you. What other words can your child think of that start with the same sound as *quilt*? Have your child trace the letters with his or her finger before using a pencil to complete the activity.

Trace a letter.

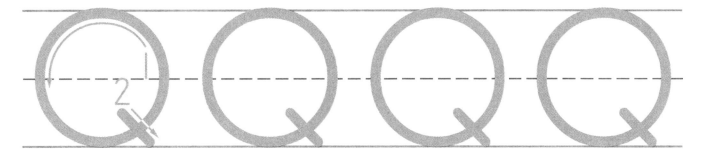

Q is for quilt.

R Is for Rabbit

Directions: Say the letter name out loud and have your child repeat you. What other words can your child think of that start with the same sound as *rabbit*? Have your child trace the letters with his or her finger before using a pencil to complete the activity.

Trace a letter.

R is for **rabbit.**

S Is for Sun

Directions: Say the letter name out loud and have your child repeat you. What other words can your child think of that start with the same sound as *sun*? Have your child trace the letters with his or her finger before using a pencil to complete the activity.

Trace a letter.

S is for sun.

T Is for Tent

Directions: Say the letter name out loud and have your child repeat you. What other words can your child think of that start with the same sound as *tent*? Have your child trace the letters with his or her finger before using a pencil to complete the activity.

Trace a letter.

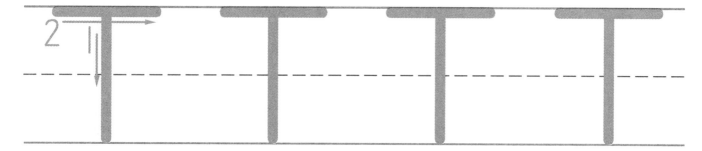

T is for tent.

U Is for Umbrella

Directions: Say the letter name out loud and have your child repeat you. What other words can your child think of that start with the same sound as *umbrella*? Have your child trace the letters with his or her finger before using a pencil to complete the activity.

Trace a letter.

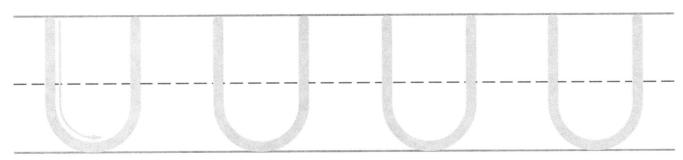

U is for umbrella.

V **Is for Vase**

Directions: Say the letter name out loud and have your child repeat you. What other words can your child think of that start with the same sound as *vase*? Have your child trace the letters with his or her finger before using a pencil to complete the activity.

Trace a letter.

V **is for** vase.

W **Is for Wagon**

Directions: Say the letter name out loud and have your child repeat you. What other words can your child think of that start with the same sound as *wagon*? Have your child trace the letters with his or her finger before using a pencil to complete the activity.

Trace a letter.

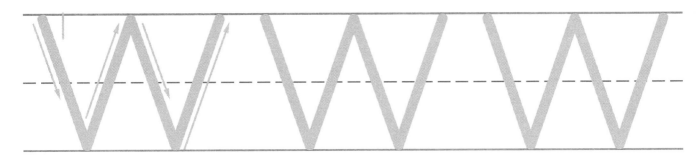

W is for wagon.

X Is for X-Ray

Directions: Say the letter name out loud and have your child repeat you. What other words can your child think of that start with the same sound as *X-ray*? Have your child trace the letters with his or her finger before using a pencil to complete the activity.

Trace a letter.

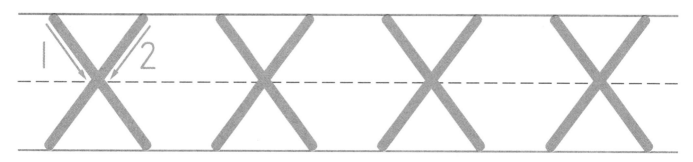

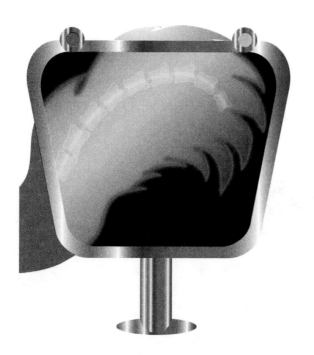

X is for X-ray.

Y **Is for Yo-Yo**

Directions: Say the letter name out loud and have your child repeat you. What other words can your child think of that start with the same sound as *yo-yo*? Have your child trace the letters with his or her finger before using a pencil to complete the activity.

Trace a letter.

Y is for yo-yo.

ACTIVITY 26

Z Is for Zoo

Directions: Say the letter name out loud and have your child repeat you. What other words can your child think of that start with the same sound as *zoo*? Have your child trace the letters with his or her finger before using a pencil to complete the activity.

Trace a letter.

Z is for zoo.

Trace Aa to Zz

Directions: Have your child point to each letter of the alphabet and say its name. Encourage your child to trace each letter with his or her finger. Then, have your child trace each letter with a crayon.

Say the letters. Trace the letters.

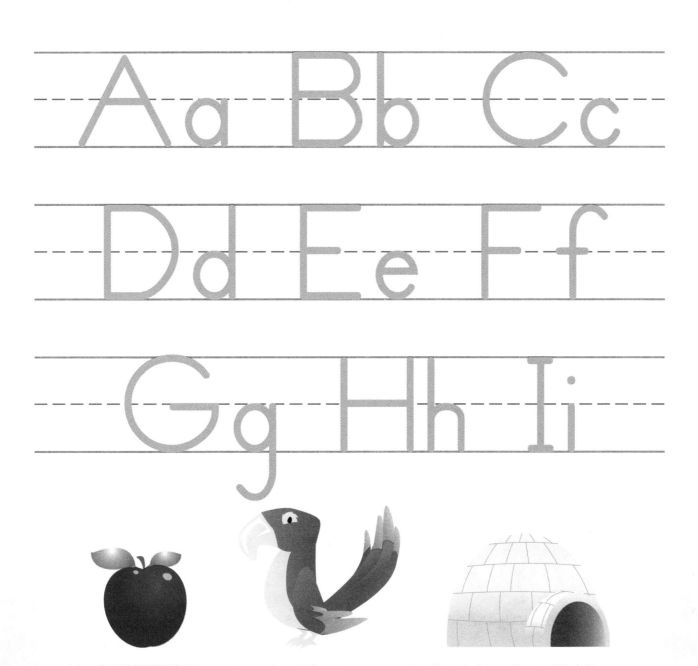

Trace Aa to Zz

Directions: Have your child point to each letter of the alphabet and say its name. Encourage your child to trace each letter with his or her finger. Then, have your child trace each letter with a crayon.

Say the letters. Trace the letters.

Trace Aa to Zz

Directions: Have your child point to each letter of the alphabet and say its name. Encourage your child to trace each letter with his or her finger. Then, have your child trace each letter with a crayon.

Say the letters. Trace the letters.

ACTIVITY 30

The Name Game

Directions: Have your child write his or her first name on the line. Help your child write the name of a friend, sibling, or pet. Spell the name letter by letter. Have your child write each letter as you say it.

Write the letters.

My name is

My friend's name is